美國權利法案

How We Organize Ourselves | Non-Fiction Series

Copyright © 2022 by Level Learning, INC. and Washington Yu Ying PCS™
Original and Edited Text Copyright © 2022 by Washington Yu Ying PCS™

All rights reserved. No part of this book in whole or part may be reproduced without written permission from the publisher.

Published by Level Learning, INC.

Content Contributors:
Washington Yu Ying PCS™ - Aini Fang, Pearl Zao He You
Level Learning - Jingyao Qi

Illustrations by: Josh Taira

Leveling classification based on Level Learning standard. For full description, visit www.levellearning.com

ISBN 978-1-64040-130-3
Traditional Chinese Edition

About Level Learning:
Level Learning provides a literacy focused curriculum specifically designed for K-12 Chinese as a Second Language classrooms. Our program offers 20 levels of specific and detailed objectives, leveled texts and passages, mastery-based online assessment, and analytics to enable data-driven instruction. Level Learning reading curriculum for both literature and informational text emphasize grammar and comprehension skills to help teachers develop confident and independent Chinese language readers. The non-fiction series of books are specifically designed to support our informational text course based on multiple national standards. To learn more about our entire offering, visit www.levellearning.com.

About Washington Yu Ying PCS™:
Washington Yu Ying PCS is a Mandarin English dual language immersion International Baccalaureate (IB) World school. Yu Ying's mission is to inspire and prepare young people to create a better world by challenging them to reach their full potential in a nurturing Chinese/English educational environment. Yu Ying's comprehensive IB, dual immersion curriculum equips students with global competencies for success in the real world. As a leader in immersion education, Yu Ying is determined to advance Chinese language programs and global citizenry education by helping other schools create and strengthen their Chinese programs. For more information, email: products@washingtonyuying.org

什麼是美國權利法案？美國憲法有27條修正案。美國權利法案是美國憲法的前10條修正案。

JAMES MADISON
詹姆士·麥迪遜

1789年，美國國會一共提出了12條修正案。 1791年12月15日，這12條修正案中的10條被通過了。這10條修正案就是美國權利法案。

美國權利法案以保護公民權利為主。其中的第一條和第四條尤其和人們的生活息息相關。

美國權利法案第一條修正案：

人們的宗教和言論自由受到保護。

這一條修正案的意思是：人們有權利選擇或改變自己的宗教信仰，這就是宗教自由。有的人信佛教、有的人信基督教、也有的人信伊斯蘭教等。當然，你也可以選擇沒有宗教信仰。

人們也可以自由地說出自己的想法,這就是言論自由。但是,你的言論不能給其他人造成傷害。比如說,在沒有火災的時候,如果你大叫「著火啦,快逃啊!」這可能會引起恐慌,造成傷害。這就不是言論自由的一部分了。

美國權利法案第四條修正案：人們的人身和財產不可以受到沒有理由的搜查。

在1791年權利法案被通過的時候，這條修正案裡的人身和財產還只是代表一個人的身體、房子、車子等。但是，隨著科學技術的發展，人們在網絡上創造了另一個世界。每天都有成千上萬人把自己的個人信息或照片放在網絡上，同時，這些信息也被以各種各樣的方式傳播或使用著。這樣算是違法嗎？網絡信息是不是應該算作人身財產而受到保護呢？

什麼是合法？什麼是違法？法官們需要根據權利法案第四條，也根據不同的情況做出判斷。

如果你有機會來首都華盛頓旅遊，一定要去參觀一下美國國家檔案館。在那裡展示著美國權利法案的原稿哦！

Glossary

	Pinyin	English Definition
權利法案	quán lì fǎ àn	Bill of Rights
憲法	xiàn fǎ	constitution
修正案	xiū zhèng àn	amendment
以……為主	yǐ……wéi zhǔ	as main focus
保護	bǎo hù	to protect
公民權利	gōng mín quán lì	civil rights
尤其	yóu qí	especially
息息相關	xī xī xiāng guān	closely related
宗教	zōng jiào	religious
言論	yán lùn	speech
自由	zì yóu	freedom
受到	shòu dào	to receive
宗教信仰	zōng jiào xìn yǎng	religious belief
佛教	fó jiào	Buddhism
基督教	jī dū jiào	Christianity

	Pinyin	English Definition
伊斯蘭教	yī sī lán jiào	Islam
當然	dāng rán	certainly
比如	bǐ rú	such as
引起	yǐn qǐ	to cause
恐慌	kǒng huāng	panic
造成	zào chéng	to cause
財產	cái chǎn	property
理由	lǐ yóu	reason
搜查	sōu chá	to search
代表	dài biǎo	to represent
網絡	wǎng luò	Internet
信息	xìn xī	information
傳播	chuán bō	to spread
違法	wéi fǎ	to break the law
合法	hé fǎ	lawful, legal

Glossary

	Pinyin	English Definition
根據	gēn jù	according to
判斷	pàn duàn	judgement
首都	shǒu dū	capital
參觀	cān guān	to visit
國家檔案館	guó jiā dàng àn guǎn	National Archives
原稿	yuán gǎo	manuscript, original copy

www.ingramcontent.com/pod-product-compliance
Lightning Source LLC
LaVergne TN
LVHW070047070526
838200LV00028B/411